SAVE IT FOR LATER

DONNA TAGLIABRACCI

Illustrations by Angelea Rivers

Save it for Later

iUniverse books may be ordered through booksellers or by contacting:

iUniverse
1663 Liberty Drive
Bloomington, IN 47403
www.iuniverse.com
1-800-Authors (1-800-288-4677)

Because of the dynamic nature of the Internet, any web addresses or links contained in this book may have changed since publication and may no longer be valid. The views expressed in this work are solely those of the author and do not necessarily reflect the views of the publisher, and the publisher hereby disclaims any responsibility for them.

Any people depicted in stock imagery provided by Getty Images are models, and such images are being used for illustrative purposes only.
Certain stock imagery © Getty Images.

ISBN: 978-1-5320-7511-7 (sc)
ISBN: 978-1-5320-7512-4 (e)

Print information available on the last page.

iUniverse rev. date: 07/29/2019

In memory of Pat Chapman

After spending the morning cleaning the barn for the miniature horses at Grampas', it was time to stop for lunch.

Lunches were usually pretty good because Nana Jo made sure that she made something special. Today was sandwich day, grampas' favourite, made with fresh buns.

Grampas' eyes were not so good any more but that was not actually the problem. The problem was that he didn't pay attention to what was going into his mouth. Phil noticed that it looked like there was a moth on grampas' shirt. "Grampa, there's something on your shirt", said Phil. Grampa looked down; saw something yellow, and he thought it was a piece of bun. He said "Saving it for later", but then quickly changed his mind and put it into his mouth. Phil looked at him in disgust. "Grampa, I think that was a moth". "That was gross", said Brett.

The next morning, after the chores were done, Nana Jo made pancakes and sausage for breakfast. Phil and Brett were at the table with Grampa and Nana Jo eating the delicious pancakes. Phil was intently watching a giant spider crawling up the tablecloth towards Grampas' plate. Then it was on the plate and on Grampas' fork. "Grampa", Phil yelled. It was too late! It went into Grampas' mouth. "That was a spider" he said. Phil looked at Grampa in disgust. Brett said "That was gross". Grampa didn't even notice.

After that, there was a mandatory fishing tournament. It was every man for himself at the pond behind the house. They fished for small mouthed bass. Brett won the tournament with the biggest fish. He was very proud. To celebrate they had a snack of Nana Jos' homemade chocolate chip cookies and a glass of milk. Phil and Brett were sitting outside with Grampa and Nana Jo at the picnic table. It happened to be tent caterpillar season and guess what! One fell off the tree onto Grampas' cookie and was going into Grampas' mouth. Phil yelled "Grampa". It was too late. "Grampa, you just ate a caterpillar." Phil watched his cookie very carefully to make sure no caterpillars went on his cookie. He looked at Grampa in disgust. Brett said, "That was gross."

That night they were having spaghetti and meatballs and salad for supper. Phil was very hungry. Phil was the only one who really liked salad so he loaded up half of his plate with salad and then the other half with spaghetti and meatballs. Brett just had spaghetti and meatballs. All of a sudden Grampa yelled, "Phil that was a green caterpillar in your salad." It was too late. It was already in Phils' mouth. Phil ran to the sink and spit out the lettuce. Sure enough there was the caterpillar. Grampa looked at Phil in disgust. Brett said, "That was gross." Then Grampa smiled.

As always the summer was filled with adventure for the grandchildren. Each day was pretty exciting with grampa.

Printed in the United States
By Bookmasters